NOV   2012

The Technology of Farming

Producing Fruits

Lori McManus

Chicago, Illinois

www.capstonepub.com
Visit our website to find out more information about Heinemann-Raintree books.

To order:
☎ Phone 888-454-2279

🖥 Visit www.capstonepub.com to browse our catalog and order online.

© 2013 Heinemann Library
an imprint of Capstone Global Library, LLC
Chicago, Illinois

Edited by Abby Colich, Megan Cotugno, and Nancy Dickmann
Designed by Victoria Allen
Picture research by Elizabeth Alexander
Illustrations by Oxford Designers and Illustrators

Originated by Capstone Global Library Ltd
Printed and bound in China by China Translation and Printing Services Ltd

16 15 14 13 12
10 9 8 7 6 5 4 3 2 1

Library of Congress Cataloging-in-Publication Data

McManus, Lori.
  Producing fruits / Lori McManus.—1st ed.
    p. cm.—(The technology of farming)
  Includes bibliographical references and index.
  ISBN 978-1-4329-6408-5 (hb)—ISBN 978-1-4329-6415-3 (pb)
1. Fruit—Juvenile literature. 2. Fruit-culture—Juvenile literature. I. Title. II. Series: Technology of farming.
  SB354.8.M36 2012
  634—dc23
  2011037567

Acknowledgments

We would like to thank the following for permission to reproduce photographs: Alamy: pp. 19 (© GFC Collection), 29 (© Global Warming Images), 32 (© Pierre BRYE), 35 (© jiashu xu); Getty Images: pp. 17 (SambaPhoto/Geyson Magno), 23 (SAID KHATIB/AFP), 24 (Hulton Archive), 27 (ROMEO GACAD/AFP), 41 (ROMEO GACAD/AFP); iStockphoto: p. 36 (© yungshu chao); Photolibrary: pp. 9 (Toshihiko Watanabe), 13 (FogStock LLC), 30 (Philippe Rocher), 31 (Stéphane OUZOUNOFF); Shutterstock: pp. 5 (© Margarita Borodina), 7 (© AnutkaT), 10 (© AJP), 14 (© Oleksii Sagitov), 15 (© Aaron Amat), 18 (© flypig), 21 (© Phillip Minnis), 25 (© Maresol), 33 (© Truyen Vu), 39 (© Gautier Willaume); © Vision Robotics Corporation: p. 42.

Cover photo of workers washing bananas reproduced with permission from Photolibrary (Imagesource).

Every effort has been made to contact copyright holders of any material reproduced in this book. Any omissions will be rectified in subsequent printings if notice is given to the publisher.

Disclaimer

Contents

What Is Fruit Farming? 4

When Did Fruit Farming Begin? 8

How Did Fruit Farming Spread Around the World? 12

Where Are Fruit Farms Located Today? 16

What Does It Take to Produce Fruit Crops? 22

How Are Fruit Crops Harvested? 28

What Methods Make Fruit Farming Sustainable? 34

What Will Happen to Fruit Farming in the Future? 40

Glossary 44

Find Out More 46

Index 48

Some words appear in the text in bold, **like this**. You can find out what they mean by looking in the glossary.

What Is Fruit Farming?

What is your favorite kind of fruit to eat? It can be hard to choose among so many delicious varieties: juicy strawberries, sweet cherries, cool watermelon, crunchy apples, and fresh peaches. Fruits not only taste good, but they also provide important vitamins and energy for the body.

Farmers all over the world grow the fruit found in markets and grocery stores. Fruit farming requires knowledge about plants, careful attention to growing conditions, and **technology** to assist with the farming process. Some fruit farming methods are more helpful to people and the **environment** than others.

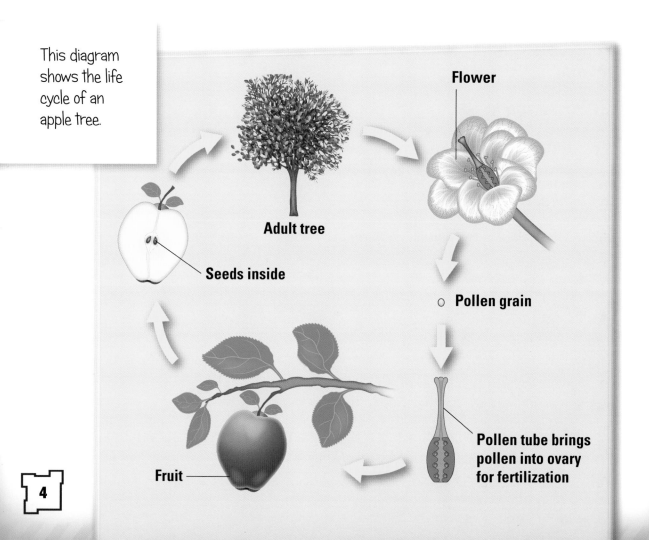

This diagram shows the life cycle of an apple tree.

Flower

Adult tree

Seeds inside

○ **Pollen grain**

Fruit

Pollen tube brings pollen into ovary for fertilization

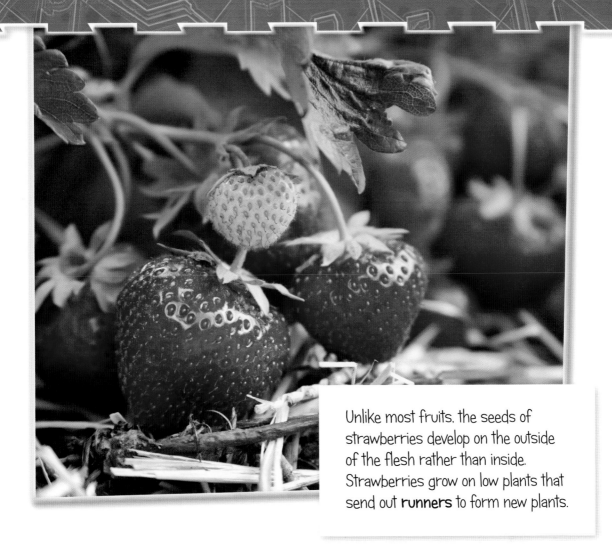

Unlike most fruits, the seeds of strawberries develop on the outside of the flesh rather than inside. Strawberries grow on low plants that send out **runners** to form new plants.

How does fruit grow?

Fruit grows naturally on some plants as part of the plant's **life cycle**. The fruit develops from a flower and contains the plant's seeds or pit. The plump **flesh** of the fruit protects the seeds so they can eventually become new plants. Most fruit-producing plants live longer than a year. For example, peach trees produce fruit for 8 to 20 years.

Some fruits grow on trees. Tree fruits include apples, pears, plums, apricots, oranges, and cherries. Some fruits grow on vines, like grapes and melons. Blueberries and raspberries grow on bushes. Bananas grow on a plant that is tall but is considered an herb rather than a tree, because it does not have a trunk made of wood.

Where does fruit grow?

Fruit grows all over the world. But certain kinds of fruit grow best in specific **climates**. For example, pineapples grow best with warm weather all year and plenty of rain. The type of weather in a location helps a farmer determine what type of fruit **crop** to grow.

Fruit farms have different names depending on the type of fruit being grown. Fruit farms with trees planted in long rows are called orchards. Farms that grow grapes are called vineyards. Bananas are grown on farms called plantations.

Technology in fruit farming

Fruit farming began over 8,000 years ago. Since that time farmers have used a variety of tools, equipment, and methods to help their fruit crops grow. Some tools, such as the **plow**, have been used for thousands of years. Other farming methods are very new, like using robots to pick strawberries.

Today fruit farmers have many choices of tools and methods. For example, farmers can use powerful chemicals to keep insects from ruining fruit crops. The chemicals work well, but they can have negative effects on the environment and people. Some farmers choose to release ladybugs instead. The ladybugs feed on the harmful insects.

Bees transfer pollen from part of one flower to another, an important step in the development of fruit.

Bees

Farmers often use bees to **pollinate** fruit trees. The bees are released among the trees in spring when the flowers are open. In recent years, the wild bee population has decreased significantly due to diseases. Farmers use bees that have been raised by trained beekeepers.

When Did Fruit Farming Begin?

Fruit farming began between 6000 and 3000 BCE. Ancient art, written records, and remains of fruit found at ancient locations have helped scientists determine these dates.

The beginning of agriculture

Before 10,000 BCE, ancient people moved from place to place to find food. They hunted animals, caught fish, and collected fruit where it grew naturally. **Agriculture** began around 9500 BCE, when people started raising animals and growing plants for food. Fruit farming started around 6000 BCE with **crops** such as figs, plums, and grapes.

Evidence from the ancient world

Fruit farming began in the ancient **civilizations** of Mesopotamia and Egypt. In present-day Iran, scientists have found the remains of grapes inside clay pots dating back to 5000 BCE. Egyptian tomb paintings from 1900 BCE show monkeys helping farmers pick fruit from trees.

People in ancient India and China also grew fruit crops. Mangoes and oranges were farmed in these areas by 3000 BCE. Bananas appear in wall paintings in India from around 450 BCE. By 200 BCE the ancient Chinese civilization had become wealthy from agriculture. Books from the Han dynasty in China (206 BCE –220 CE) record information on protecting peach and mandarin orange trees from insects.

Figs were one of the first **cultivated** fruit crops. Fig trees grow about 30 feet (9 meters) high and produce two or three crops of fruit each year.

Plow

A **plow** is a tool that breaks up soil and prepares it for planting. Plows were invented in the Middle East soon after agriculture began. The earliest plows, called ards, were probably made from sharpened tree branches. They were pulled by two oxen so that the animals' strength could be used to turn over the soil. In the 1800s, factories began producing metal plows. After 1860, plows could be pulled by steam engines instead of animals. Today metal plows are pulled behind tractors.

What about water?

Growing fruit trees and grapevines requires plenty of water. Ancient people invented **irrigation** systems to provide regular water for crops. The Mesopotamians built the first simple irrigation system around 7000 BCE. The earliest large-scale irrigation system was created around 4000 BCE in southern Russia. This system had **canals** up to 10 feet (3 meters) across and more than a mile (1.6 kilometers) long!

Many farmers in poor countries still use simple plows pulled by animals.

By 2800 BCE the Egyptian government hired people specifically to build and supervise irrigation systems. Written records show the Egyptians built a 350-foot-long (106-meter-long) **dam** on the Nile River around 2500 BCE to control the flow of water. Irrigation was being used in China by 2200 BCE.

Farmers in ancient Greece built small dams across streams and brought up water from wells so they could grow fruit crops. In *The Odyssey*, written around 700 BCE, the famous Greek poet Homer describes pear, pomegranate, apple, and fig trees growing well in Greece.

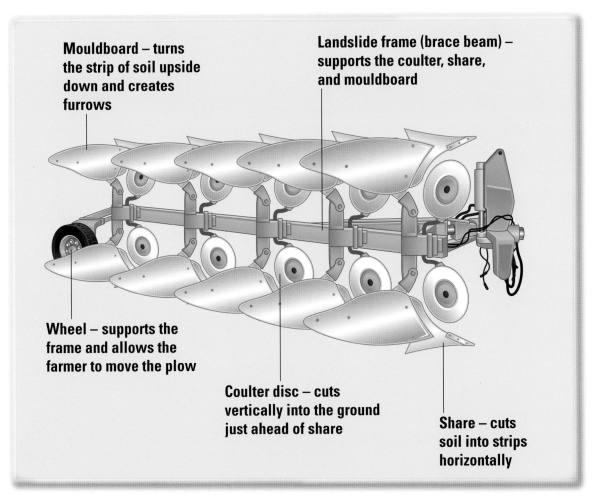

Mouldboard – turns the strip of soil upside down and creates furrows

Landslide frame (brace beam) – supports the coulter, share, and mouldboard

Wheel – supports the frame and allows the farmer to move the plow

Coulter disc – cuts vertically into the ground just ahead of share

Share – cuts soil into strips horizontally

Modern plows are lowered and raised hydraulically—using liquids under pressure.

How Did Fruit Farming Spread Around the World?

Fruit farming spread as people traveled to different areas around the world. Countries sent individuals and armies to explore, trade with, and conquer other nations. The adventurers often brought fruit seeds and young plants back to their homelands. Farmers made changes to their land so that they could grow new types of fruit.

The early centuries of the Common Era

In the Roman Republic (500–27 BCE), grapes, apples, and plums were common **crops** around the Mediterranean Sea. As the Roman Empire (27 BCE–476 CE) expanded, farmers planted new fruit crops such as cherries, apricots, and peaches introduced by travelers. Roman sea traders brought home young orange trees from India around 100 CE.

After 600 CE, Arab armies began taking control of lands in North Africa, the Middle East, and Asia, creating an Arab Empire. Farming techniques and fruit crops spread to new areas. In 644 CE, Arab scientists developed a windmill to pump water for **irrigation**. By 1000 CE, Arabs introduced **fertilizers** to enrich farm soil. About this time, Arab traders introduced mango trees to North Africa.

Curved Harvest Knife

Knives have been used for thousands of years to cut **ripe** fruit off vines. Even today farmworkers use special curved knives to **harvest** grapes, strawberries, and melons such as cantaloupe and honeydew. Harvesting by hand prevents damage to the fruit. Also, many farmers cannot afford to buy expensive harvesting machines.

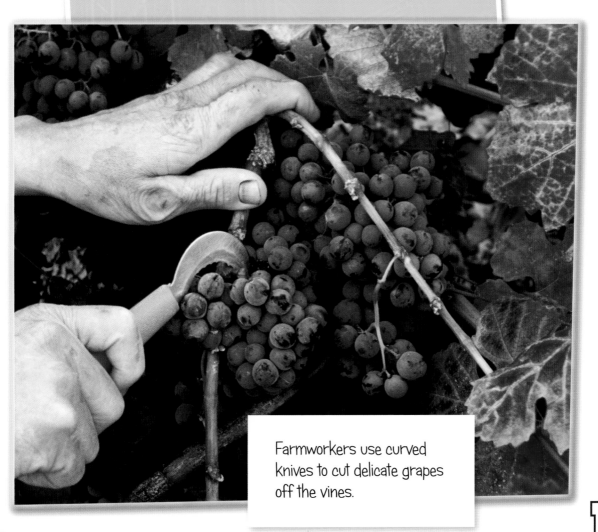

Farmworkers use curved knives to cut delicate grapes off the vines.

The age of exploration spreads fruit

From the early 1400s to the 1700s, ocean ships became stronger and safer. European countries sent citizens to explore and establish trading relationships with countries in Africa, Asia, South America, and the Caribbean. During this time, fruit seeds and plants traveled across oceans to new locations.

Brought over from the Caribbean, the pineapple became popular in Europe and Asia by the mid-1500s. Melons were introduced in Mexico and South America by Spanish explorers. Spaniards also brought peaches to Florida, where farming peaches became popular with American Indians. The practice of farming grapes spread from Europe to Africa, Australia, and the Americas between 1500 and 1800.

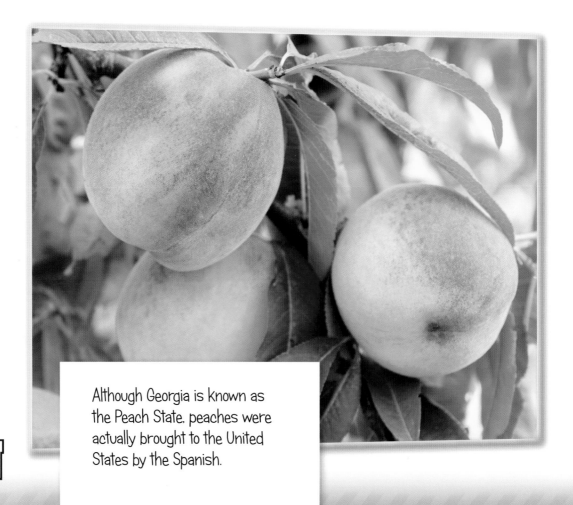

Although Georgia is known as the Peach State, peaches were actually brought to the United States by the Spanish.

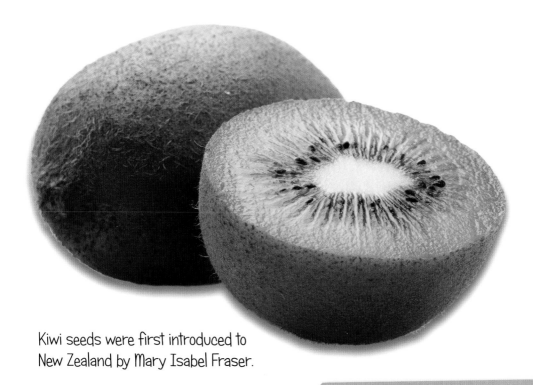

Kiwi seeds were first introduced to New Zealand by Mary Isabel Fraser.

Changing the land

Not all fruit crops grew well if the new location was very different from the old one. Farmers often cleared trees or drained water from soggy areas to make planting crops possible. Soil was poured into low areas to flatten the land. Farmers sometimes built **greenhouses** or walls around gardens to grow warm-weather crops in colder **climates**.

Mary Isabel Fraser (1863–1942)

In the early 1900s, Mary Isabel Fraser visited China and tasted kiwifruit (or kiwi) for the first time. She brought kiwi seeds back home to New Zealand. With the help of a gardener, Fraser grew the first New Zealand crop of kiwi in 1910. Today the country of New Zealand produces one-third of the world's supply of kiwi.

Where Are Fruit Farms Located Today?

Fruit farms are located all over the world. For best growth, specific **crops** are matched to the **climate** and the growing conditions of an area. Today farmers can improve conditions through **irrigation**, **fertilizers**, and **cover crops**.

Tropical fruits

The **equator** is located in Earth's tropical climate zone. The tropical zone has warm weather with plenty of rain all year. Fruits such as pineapples, persimmons, papayas, and bananas grow best in this climate.

Bananas are the number-one fruit crop in the world. They grow in more than 100 countries on farms called plantations. India grows more bananas than any other country. The Philippines, China, and Ecuador are the next three top **producers** of bananas.

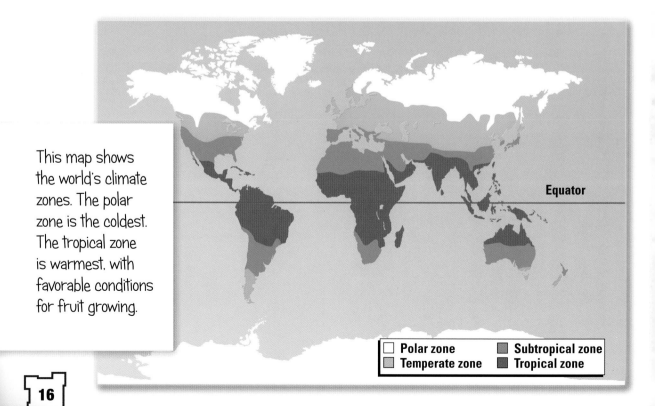

This map shows the world's climate zones. The polar zone is the coldest. The tropical zone is warmest, with favorable conditions for fruit growing.

Equator

Polar zone | Subtropical zone
Temperate zone | Tropical zone

Subtropical fruits

Some fruits grow best in the subtropical climate zone (see map). The subtropical zone has mild weather and typically does not experience frost during winter. Fruits that grow best in a subtropical climate include pomegranates, guava, lemons, and grapefruits. Oranges are the most-grown subtropical fruit crop in the world. Brazil grows more oranges than any other country. The United States is the second-largest producer of oranges.

Harvest Bins

When fruits are **harvested** by hand, they are immediately placed in plastic, cardboard, cloth, or woven bins. These bins are then transported to indoor locations. Often bins are rectangular so they can be stacked on top of one another. Some bins are so large they must be lifted by machine.

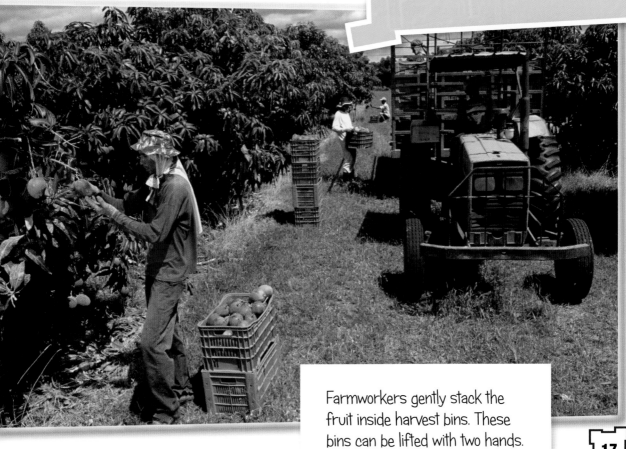

Farmworkers gently stack the fruit inside harvest bins. These bins can be lifted with two hands.

Temperate climate zone

The Earth's temperate climate zone has weather that varies with the seasons. Summers are hot and winters are cold. Pears, peaches, apricots, plums, cherries, blueberries, and raspberries grow in the temperate zone.

Apples are also a common temperate fruit. More than 6,000 different kinds of apples are grown around the world. The biggest producer of apples is China. The United States, Iran, Turkey, Russia, Italy, and India also grow large crops of apples.

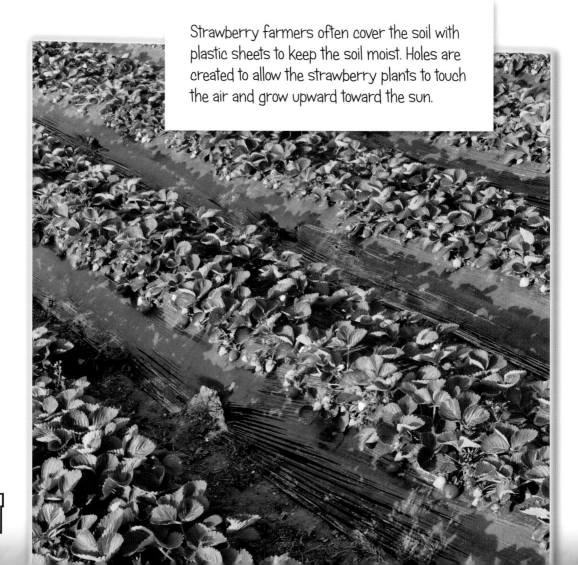

Strawberry farmers often cover the soil with plastic sheets to keep the soil moist. Holes are created to allow the strawberry plants to touch the air and grow upward toward the sun.

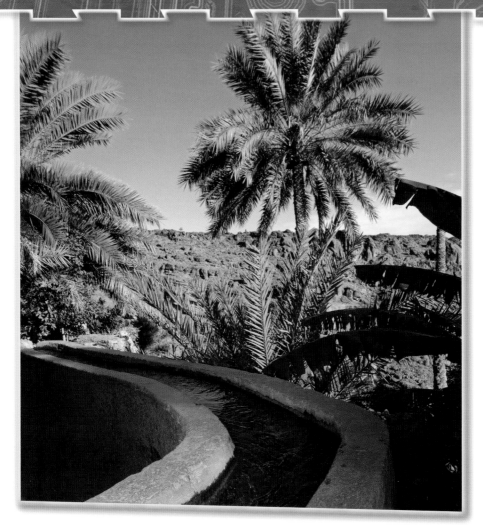

Water evaporates quickly from the large leaves of date palms. Farmers create irrigation systems to be sure date palms get enough water to grow sweet fruit.

Growing conditions

Why is a certain location selected for fruit farming? Besides climate, farmers also consider how the growing conditions will affect a particular fruit crop. These conditions include the type of soil and water supply in the area. Farmers also consider the **elevation**, the shape of the land, and the amount of time it will take to transport a delicate fruit to a market.

Farmers can improve the conditions of an area by using science-based tools. For example, strawberries grow best in **moist** soil. If the area does not get enough rain, farmers use irrigation lines to provide an ongoing supply of water. Many strawberry farmers also cover the soil with plastic so the water stays in the soil instead of **evaporating** into the air.

Caring for the soil

Fruit crops grow best in soil containing **nutrients**. If the soil lacks certain nutrients, a farmer will often apply a fertilizer. A farmer may also choose to grow a cover crop, such as beans or oats. Instead of using these plants as food for people, the farmer plows the cut crops into the soil. When the plants break down, they provide nutrients to the soil. Then the fruit can be grown in healthy soil.

If fruit crops are planted on hillsides or windy areas, farmers must prevent soil **erosion**. Often cover crops are grown around fruit trees to keep the soil in place. For example, a farmer may grow grass between orange trees grown on hills. Farmers may also plant tall, dense trees at the edges of a fruit farm. These trees provide a **windbreak**, which helps prevent soil erosion.

Tractors

Farmers use tractors to push and pull heavy loads. Tractors were invented in the 1880s to pull **plows** through fields. By the 1920s, the all-purpose, modern tractor had been developed. With different attachments, tractors can now be used for plowing, planting, **cultivating**, mowing, harvesting, and moving soil or heavy equipment. Farmers who cannot afford tractors or have small fields still use animals to push and pull equipment.

Modern tractors have thick, oversized tires
to allow movement over uneven ground.

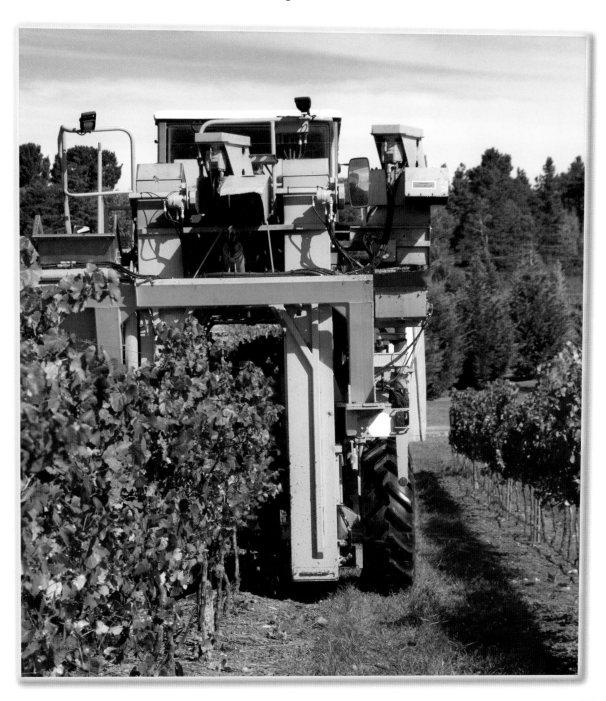

What Does It Take to Produce Fruit Crops?

Farmers work hard to produce fruit **crops** with specific flavors, sizes, and shapes. Crops must be planted, tended, and protected from animals and extreme weather. Farmers make decisions about how far apart and how tall to grow plants. They must also decide whether to use chemicals.

Propagating fruit crops

Fruit farmers rarely plant seeds in a field in order to grow new crops. Fruit crops are **propagated** in other ways. Some fruit-producing plants are grown from cuttings. Cuttings are sections of another plant that are cut off and planted in the soil. The cuttings then grow roots and eventually become fully developed plants. Fruit crops that grow well from cuttings include grapes and blueberries.

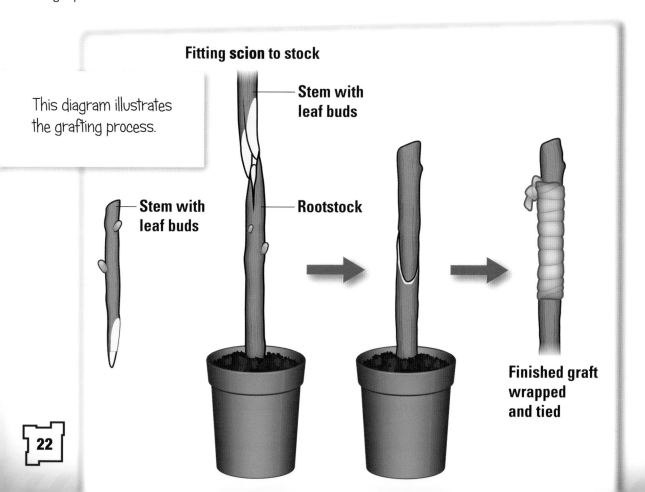

Fitting scion to stock

This diagram illustrates the grafting process.

Stem with leaf buds

Stem with leaf buds

Rootstock

Finished graft wrapped and tied

In a nursery, farmers carefully control the temperature, sunlight, water, and soil **nutrients**.

Many fruit trees do not grow strong roots easily. These trees are propagated most often by grafting (see diagram on page 22). Grafting involves inserting a stem with leaf buds into the rootstock (lower part of the trunk) of a young tree. Eventually the stem becomes part of the tree and produces fruit. Grafting is used to propagate specific types of apples, pears, peaches, and other tree fruits.

Plants grown from cuttings or by grafting often spend one to two years in a **nursery** before being planted in a field. In a nursery young plants receive special daily attention. Young plants grown from **runners**, such as strawberries and raspberries, also spend time in nurseries before being planted in fields.

Just the right fruit

People and companies who buy fruit often want the fruit to have a certain appearance or taste. Farmers use **selective breeding** to propagate plants with the desired characteristics. For example, a farmer may graft new apple trees so that only apples with bright red skin are produced. Another farmer might choose to propagate only vines that grow seedless grapes.

Luther Burbank (1849–1926)

American Luther Burbank studied plants and plant cultivation. He developed more than 800 new plant varieties by using selective breeding and grafting. In 1893 Burbank published a book titled *New Creations in Fruit and Flowers*. In the book he listed and described his best varieties.

Luther Burbank created new varieties of plums, pears, blackberries, raspberries, strawberries, cherries, apples, grapes, and nectarines.

Farming decisions

Many farming decisions affect fruit characteristics. Each farmer must decide how close together to place the individual plants in the field. Planting farther apart means the crop will contain fewer trees and fewer fruits, but the fruits will be larger. Planting closer together produces smaller fruit on more trees.

The tallest, biggest trees or bushes do not always yield the most fruit. Controlling the height of plants helps produce more fruit in less space. Farmers may also change a tree's shape by cutting branches or forcing branches to grow in a certain direction. The shape of the tree affects its lifespan and the size of its fruit.

Apricot trees can be trained to grow against frames. The apricots receive more sunlight and produce plumper fruit when the trees are shaped this way.

Protecting fruit crops

Farmers actively protect their crops from danger. Some fruits will stop developing or die if the temperature gets too cold. Farmers may use metal heaters or small fires in their fields during cold spells to prevent frost. Other farmers may place fabric over the plants to keep heat around them.

Animals may try to eat the fruit while it is growing. Farmers often place fences or netting around crops to protect them from land animals such as deer and foxes. Birds can approach crops from the sky. Farmers use stuffed scarecrows, netting, and machines to keep birds away.

Diseases and insects can also damage fruit crops. Farmers take action against these dangers by using **pesticides**. Some pesticides are made from chemicals. Others are made from natural materials. Pesticides can also help kill weeds that a farmer does not want growing in the field. Weeds use up important soil nutrients and water intended for the fruit crop.

Crop Duster

Did you know that some airplanes are farm vehicles? Crop dusters are airplanes that fly low to distribute **fertilizers** or pesticides on crops. Crop dusters can spray large areas in a short time period. Pilots use GPS (Global Positioning System) **technology** to plan their flying paths and record which crops have already been sprayed.

Crop dusters contain storage
tanks and use high-speed
sprayers to distribute
fertilizers or pesticides.

How Are Fruit Crops Harvested?

Many fruit **crops** are **harvested** by hand. Some machines can help with harvesting fruit. Farmers compare the cost of paying workers to the cost of buying and using machines. The size of the farm also makes a difference in how fruit is harvested. Farmers decide when to harvest based on the ripeness of the fruit.

Time to harvest

Most fruit crops are harvested when the fruit is **ripe**. A few fruits, such as bananas and pears, can be picked before they are ripe. These fruits ripen at the market or while stored. Other fruits, such as oranges and grapefruits, can stay on the tree for several months even after they ripen.

Farmers think about the journey of the fruit when timing the harvest. Will the fruit be in a market in less than a day? Will it be transported a long distance before being eaten? Fruits that will be eaten shortly after harvest are picked when they are quite ripe. Fruits are harvested as close as possible to the time of eating.

Cherry Picker

A cherry picker is a platform or large, strong basket that can be raised into the air hydraulically. Pulled by a truck or pushed by hand, the cherry picker is moved along rows of fruit trees. Cherry pickers help farmers harvest cherries as well as other tree fruits, such as peaches and oranges.

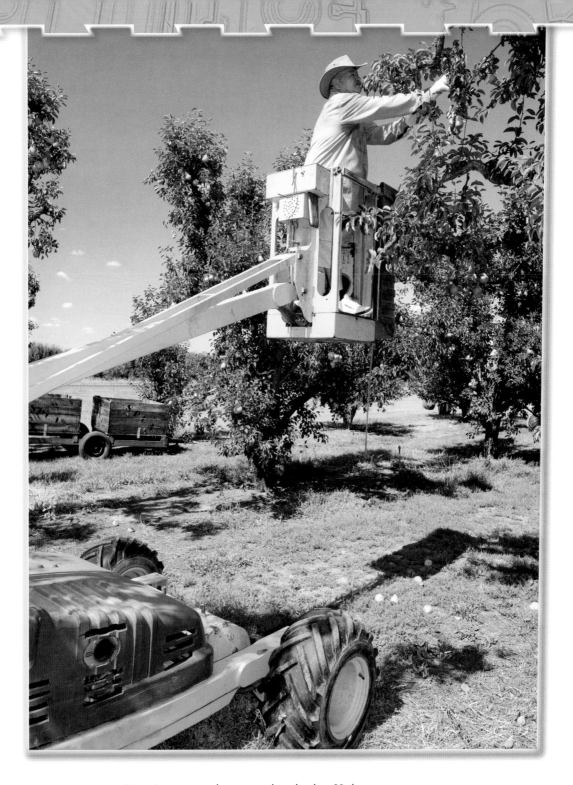

Standing on a cherry picker high off the ground, a farmworker can harvest fruits on trees with a knife or clippers.

Hand vs. machine harvesting

Berries and vine fruits such as melons and grapes are typically harvested by hand. Farmworkers use special knives or clippers to cut the fruits off the plants. These fruits are harvested by hand to prevent damage to their skin and **flesh**. Grapes are sometimes shaken off the vine by a machine, especially if they are going to be used for juice or wine.

Peaches, plums, nectarines, and other soft fruits are harvested by hand because they would be ruined if they fell to the ground.

Typically only large farms use harvest shakers. Small farms usually harvest by hand, since the machines are very expensive.

Fruits on the same bush or vine can ripen at different rates. Hand picking allows farmers to harvest only those fruits that are ripe. They leave the other fruits on the plant for a while longer.

Tree fruits are harvested in different ways. Many farmers harvest tree fruits by hand using ladders or a cherry picker and clippers. Farmers with large orchards may choose to use machines for harvesting even if some of the fruit is ruined. The time saved by using machines is worth the cost of the fruit that is lost.

Harvest Shakers

Farmers sometimes use harvest shakers to detach fruits from trees, vines, or bushes. The machine grabs part of the plant and shakes it back and forth. Ripe fruit falls into cloth sheets or frames under the trees or vines. The fruit gets bruised and will spoil if not eaten or processed quickly into juice, pies, or other fruit products.

Thinking about the costs

Farmers and companies who own farms must think about the amount of money they spend on their crops. They compare this amount to the money they hope to receive from selling the fruit. In order to continue, the farmer or company must make more money than is spent.

The biggest cost in fruit farming is either labor (people who work on the farm) or machines. People cannot work as quickly as machines, but they damage less fruit when picking it. Then more of the fruit can be sold. Small farms often rely on people because they cannot afford machines. Large farms usually use machines. The initial cost is high, but the machines cut down the time for harvesting and the money spent on labor.

Pressing fruits too close together in a container can damage the fruit. Farmers often choose packaging materials that keep fruits from touching each other.

From farm to market

Farmers and companies think about what will help their fruit crops to sell well in markets. Customers tend to buy fruit that looks good. Farmers use packaging materials like trays and plastic bags to protect the fruit. Companies sometimes spray the fruit with special ingredients to make it appear shiny and smooth.

Camlin Fine Chemicals

Based in India, Camlin Fine Chemicals produces a product for preserving fresh fruit. This product, Nanofresh, is made from natural ingredients. Nanofresh forms a coating on the skin to keep the fruit fresh longer without affecting its flavor or color.

Nanofresh can be applied to a range of fruits to keep them fresh.

What Methods Make Fruit Farming Sustainable?

Many scientists and farmers think about farming fruit in **sustainable** ways. Farmers can choose methods that improve their lives, protect the **environment**, and use **resources** carefully so fruit can be **cultivated** to feed people now and in the future.

Avoiding damage to the environment

Some methods of fruit farming negatively affect the Earth's air and water. Air pollution increases when farmers spray **pesticides** on **crops**, use certain types of **fertilizers**, or plow their fields a lot. Instead fruit farmers can choose to control pests in natural ways, such as using ladybugs. Farmers can also improve air quality by planting **windbreaks**.

Water quality is affected by farming practices. When water drains away from crops, it carries materials in the soil with it. If the soil contains chemicals from pesticides or fertilizers, those chemicals flow with the water. The water drains to creeks, rivers, and lakes. The chemicals harm the plants and animals that live in the water.

Using more natural fertilizers and pesticides can prevent water pollution. Farmers can design **irrigation** systems and use **cover crops** to keep water in the soil of their fruit fields. Planting crops along the natural shape and **elevation** of the land also helps to slow water run-off during rainstorms.

Ladybugs eat many of the insects that attack fruit. Farmers use them to control these pests.

Favorita Fruit Company

The Favorita Fruit Company is a leading banana and pineapple grower in Ecuador. The company not only grows and **exports** tropical fruit but also creates fertilizers and food packaging materials that avoid harm to the environment.

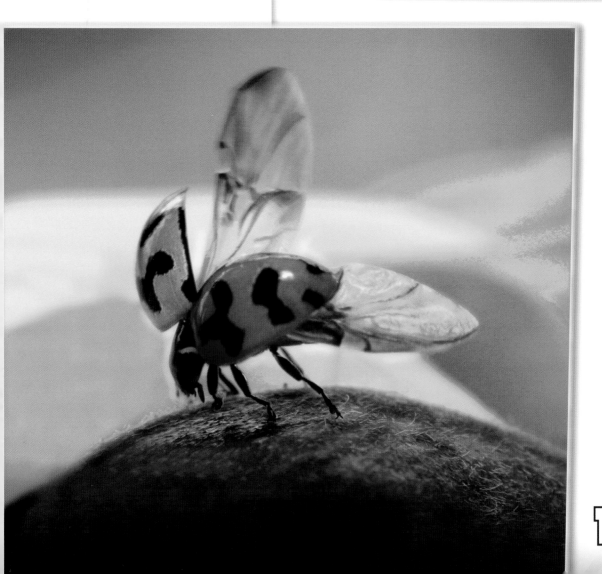

Some farmers in Kenya have recently starting growing passion fruit instead of corn. The passion fruit earns the farmers more money. A passion fruit orchard is shown here.

Soil for the future

Keeping soil healthy is an important part of sustainable fruit farming. Soil that erodes or loses **nutrients** each year will one day be unable to produce fruit crops. Farmers can plant cover crops to improve the nutrients in the soil, prevent **erosion**, and reduce weed growth. Cover crops can also help soil hold water.

Farmers may choose not to **till** the soil in order to improve its quality. "No-tillage" farming increases the amount of water and nutrients in the soil. Less plowing also reduces labor, fuel, and machine costs. Farmers must manage no-tillage crops with special care. Otherwise pest and disease problems can ruin the fruit.

Using land wisely

Farmers carefully consider how to best use their land. Some farmers choose to regularly change the type of crop they grow. This practice enhances soil nutrients and naturally stops some pests, weeds, and diseases. Some farmers choose to plant other crops in between their fruit trees. These farmers increase the amount of food produced and their **profit** from the land.

Herbert Bartz

Brazilian Herbert Bartz was the first farmer in Latin America to use no-tillage **technology.** Bartz investigated no-tillage farms in the United States and the United Kingdom, and he allowed experiments on his farm in 1971. Bartz has successfully raised no-tillage crops ever since.

Improving lives

To be sustainable, farming must improve the lives of the farmers and those in their community. Farmers need to make a profit in order to provide for their families and continue farming. They are more likely to make a profit if they grow several different kinds of crops on their land. Doing so reduces the risk of losing money if one crop does not grow well in a particular year.

Buying and selling food at local stores helps the community and the environment. If the farmer buys supplies at a nearby store and sells his fruit to a local restaurant, the business owners and the farmer benefit. When fruit is transported far from the farm, the **fuel** used by the trucks or airplanes releases harmful gases into the air. Reducing the distance food is transported also reduces air pollution.

Why not farm with sustainable methods?

Sustainable methods are practiced by farmers in some areas but not others. Farming companies in wealthy countries are sometimes more concerned about making a lot of money than protecting the environment. These companies continue to plow fields often and use chemical pesticides dropped from crop dusters.

In poorer countries many farmers are more concerned about their own family's hunger than improving the environment. They may not be educated about the most recent developments in sustainable farming.

Also, many developed countries demand fruit that is out of season or can't be grown in their own countries. They **import** fruit from other countries thousands of miles away. This fruit is usually transported in ways that are harmful to the environment.

Some farmers in Thailand have learned how to regularly rotate crops in their fields. The farmers are benefitting from improved soil and reduced pest problems.

What Will Happen to Fruit Farming in the Future?

Fruit farming has a history about 8,000 years long. Although some methods have remained the same over time, farmers and scientists continue to improve and advance fruit farming techniques. The near future may even include fruit-picking robots and vertical farms (see page 43) in unusual locations.

Steady advances in fruit farming

Scientists can already identify **genetic markers** in many fruits. For example, they know the sequence of genes that gives cherries a sweet flavor. This information helps farmers **propagate crops** with specific traits in a shorter period of time than ever before.

Some scientists take positive traits from other living things and introduce them to fruits. For example, scientists have discovered an arctic fish that produces a special substance to keep itself from freezing. By injecting this substance into strawberries, scientists hope to create fruits with built-in protection against cold weather. Farmers could then grow strawberries more successfully in areas that experience freezing temperatures during winter. However, most **genetically modified** (GM) foods have not yet been approved for sale in markets or grocery stores. Tests need to clarify whether these foods will be healthy or harmful for humans.

Despite these advances in science, farmers in poorer countries continue to propagate crops in ways that have worked for thousands of years. Without large amounts of money or access to new information, these farmers use simple tools and hard work to produce fruit crops that provide money for their families.

Scientists continue to work on identifying genetic markers for desirable traits in many fruit crops.

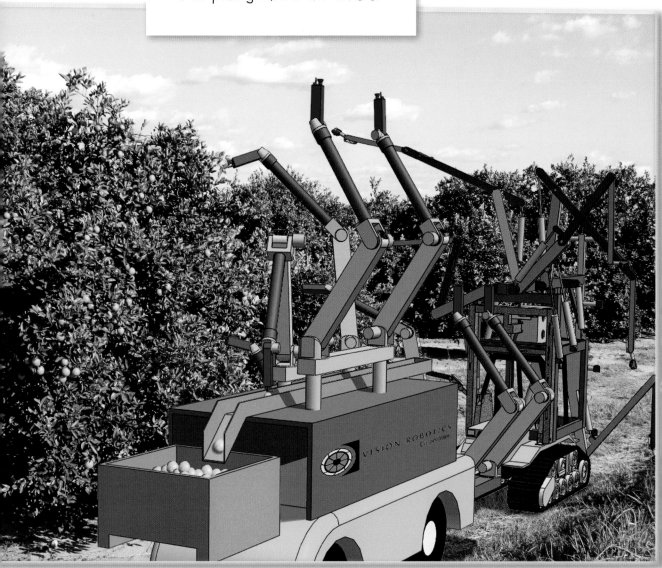

An illustration of a Vision Robotics fruit-picking robot is shown here.

Fruit-Picking Robots

One company, Vision Robotics, is developing machines that identify and harvest **ripe** fruit. The robots will move more slowly than humans because it takes time to process information about the ripeness of each fruit. However, these robots will be able to work 24 hours a day without needing breaks, food, or water. In the end, the robots will pick more fruit in less time than people. Because the robots are expensive, only very large farm companies will be able to afford them.

Looking ahead

Fruit farming may look quite different in the future. Scientists are investigating how to provide **nutrients** to plants in other ways besides soil. Perhaps in the future, dirt will not be needed to produce large fruit or vegetable crops.

Currently farmers and scientists are experimenting with vertical farms. These farms are built in skyscrapers that have many levels and glass windows on all of the walls. Each floor of the building contains crops of fruit-bearing plants or vegetables. The farming company controls almost all growing conditions, including water, nutrients, temperature, wind, and even **erosion**. The vertical farms take up little space compared to traditional farms. They can be located in almost any **climate** or location, even in cities!

When you go to the market in the future, ask the workers where and how the fruit was grown. You may find that the fruit comes from close by or thousands of miles away. Who knows—soon the answer may even be "in a skyscraper."

Glossary

agriculture organized production of crops and animals for food; farming

canal human-made waterway

civilization highly developed human society

climate general weather conditions of an area

cover crop crop planted to provide nutrients to soil or to keep soil from eroding and weeds from growing

crop food obtained from the land at the end of a season of growth

cultivate to plant, tend, and harvest plants with work and skill

dam barrier built across a stream or river to block the flow of water

elevation height of something

environment external surroundings in which a plant or animal lives

erosion process by which the surface of the earth is worn away by water, wind, waves, etc.

equator imaginary circle around the world equally distant from the north pole and south pole

evaporate to change from solid or liquid to gas

export to sell or ship to other countries

fertilizer substance added to soil to increase plant growth

flesh thick, soft part of a fruit or vegetable

fuel any substance burned as a source of heat or power, such as gasoline

genetic marker recognizable trait, gene, or DNA section used for identification

genetically modified having to do with a living thing's genes that have been changed for the purpose of improving characteristics

greenhouse building with see-through walls and roof used to grow plants under controlled conditions

harvest to gather a ripe crop

import to buy and bring in from other countries

irrigation using artificial canals and ditches to supply land with water

life cycle stages of development for a living thing, from its beginning to the time it can produce young or new plants

moist slightly wet; damp

nursery place where young trees or plants are grown in controlled conditions

nutrient substance that provides nourishment

pesticide chemical used for killing pests, especially insects

plow agricultural tool used for cutting and turning over soil

pollinate to transfer pollen from the male part of the flower to the female part

producer person, country, or thing that grows or creates products

profit income or money gained

propagate to cause a living thing to multiply or reproduce

resource source of wealth in a country, such as precious metals, healthy soil, or oil

ripe mature and ready to be eaten

runner slender stem that arches to the ground and propagates by producing new roots and shoots

scion living part of a plant that is cut off and joined to another plant

selective breeding intentionally propagating plants with desired characteristics

sustainable capable of being maintained without using up natural resources or damaging the environment

technology application of scientific knowledge for practical purposes

till to plow land for the purpose of growing crops

windbreak line of trees, fencing, etc., serving as protection from the wind

Find Out More

Books

Hendy, Jenny. *The Ultimate Step-by-Step Kids' First Gardening Book.* London: Lorenz Books, 2010.

Krezel, Cindy. *Kids' Container Gardening: Year-Round Projects for Inside and Out.* West Chicago, Ill.: Ball Publishing, 2010.

Rodger, Ellen. *Reducing Your Footprint: Farming, Cooking, and Eating for a Healthy Planet.* New York: Crabtree, 2010.

Spilsbury, Louise. *Eat Smart: Fruits.* Chicago: Heinemann Library, 2009.

Websites

Canada Agriculture Museum

Does farm equipment interest you? Explore the history of tractors, with photographs and descriptions of the machines that changed farming in Canada and around the world. This website shows different exhibits at the Canada Agriculture Museum.

www.agriculture.technomuses.ca/english/collections_research/tractors.cfm

Earthbound Farm

Earthbound Farm is a company that sells organic fruit and vegetables. Visit this website to find out more about how plants grow and how organic farmers use Earth-friendly methods to farm goods. You can download two fun activity books about using ladybugs to control pests and earthworms to keep soil healthy.

www.ebfarm.com/WhyOrganic/JustForKids.aspx

Grow Your Own

Grow fruits and vegetables in your own garden by following the tips on this website. Learn more about the parts of plants that can be eaten for food.

http://kidsgrowingstrong.com/GrowIt

Healthy Eating

On this Dole company website, you can investigate the health benefits of many fruits, such as apples, bananas, pears, apricots, and strawberries. Click on the Super Kids tab to play games and read comics about healthy eating.

www.dole.com/EatRightLanding/EatRtProductIndex/Fruits/tabid/

531/Default.aspx

Orange Pippin

This website calls itself the "comprehensive resource for apples and orchards." You can find information on different kinds of apples and locations of orchards around the United States, as well as in some other countries.

www.orangepippin.com/

Places to visit

Littletree Orchards

Newfield, New York

Pick your own apples, peaches, cherries, and pears right from the trees. Take a tour of the orchards and learn about the tree fruit growing process.

www.littletree-orchards.com

Canada Agriculture Museum

Ottawa, Ontario, Canada

Explore the sights and sounds of typical life on a farm at the Canada Agriculture Museum. Exhibits explain the essential role of bees for fruit crops and the history of the tractor.

www.agriculture.technomuses.ca/english/indexhpnagr.cfm

Index

American Indians 14
ancient farming 8, 9, 10–11, 12, 13, 14, 15, 40, 41
animals 9, 10, 20, 22, 26, 34
apples 5, 11, 12, 18, 23, 24

bananas 5, 6, 9, 16, 28, 35
Bartz, Herbert 37
bees 7
bins 17
Burbank, Luther 24

Camlin Fine Chemicals 33
chemicals 6, 22, 26, 33, 34, 38
cherry pickers 28, 31
climate 6, 15, 16, 17, 18, 22, 26, 40, 43
crop dusters 26, 38
cuttings 22, 23

diseases 7, 26, 37

elevation 19, 34
environment 4, 6, 34, 35, 38
erosion 20, 37, 43
evaporation 19

Favorita Fruit Company 35
fertilizers 12, 16, 20, 26, 34, 35
flesh 5, 30, 31
flowers 5, 7
Fraser, Mary Isabel 15

genetically modified (GM) foods 40
GPS (Global Positioning System) 26
grafting 23, 24
grapes 5, 6, 9, 10, 12, 13, 14, 22, 24, 30
growing conditions 4, 16, 19, 22, 43

harvesting 13, 17, 20, 28, 30–31, 32, 42
harvest shakers 31

insects 6, 7, 9, 26, 34
irrigation 10–11, 12, 16, 19, 34

kiwifruit 15
knives 13, 30

ladybugs 6, 34
life cycles 4, 5
lifespans 5, 25

map 16
markets 4, 19, 28, 33, 38, 40, 43
melons 5, 13, 14, 30

Nanofresh 33
New Creations in Fruit and Flowers (Luther Burbank) 24
"no-tillage" farming 37
nurseries 23
nutrients 20, 26, 37, 43

oranges 5, 9, 12, 17, 20, 28
orchards 6, 31

packaging 33, 35
peaches 5, 9, 12, 14, 18, 23, 28
pears 5, 11, 18, 23, 28
pesticides 6, 22, 26, 34, 38
pineapples 6, 14, 16, 35
plantations 6, 16
plows 6, 10, 11, 20, 34, 37, 38
pollination 7
pollution 34, 38
profit 32, 37, 38, 41
propagation 22–23, 24, 40, 41

ripeness 13, 28, 31, 42
robots 6, 42

scientists 8, 9, 12, 34, 40, 43
seeds 5, 12, 14, 15, 22, 24
selective breeding 24
soil 10, 12, 15, 19, 20, 22, 26, 34, 37, 43
spacing 25
strawberries 6, 13, 19, 23, 40
subtropical climate zone 17
sustainable methods 34, 37, 38

temperate climate zone 18
tractors 10, 20
traders 12, 14
transportation 17, 19, 28, 38
trees 5, 6, 7, 9, 10, 11, 12, 15, 20, 23, 24, 25, 28, 31, 37
tropical climate zone 16, 35

vertical farms 43
vines 5, 10, 13, 24, 30, 31
vineyards 6
Vision Robotics 42

weather 6, 15, 16, 17, 18, 22, 40
weeds 26, 37
windbreaks 20, 34
workers 13, 28, 30, 32, 37